MORNING
LEAVES

MORNING LEAVES

*Reflections on Loss,
Grief, and Connection*

LAING F. RIKKERS

Art by
KELLY LEAHY RADDING

THE
collective
BOOK STUDIO

Library of Congress Cataloging-in-Publication Data available.

ISBN: 978-1-68555-595-5
Ebook ISBN: 978-1-68555-881-9
LCCN: 2022916018

Printed using Forest Stewardship Council
certified stock from sustainably managed forests.

Manufactured in China.

Design by AJ Hansen and Kelly Leahy Radding.

10 9 8 7 6 5 4 3 2 1

The Collective Book Studio™
Oakland, California
www.thecollectivebook.studio

This book is dedicated to Ginna
who abruptly left too early.
Cracked me open.
And whispered *today*.
Now.

TABLE OF CONTENTS

MORNING LEAVES

INTRODUCTION

I distinctly recall the point of no return, that moment of truth. My sixteen-year-old daughter asked, "Is your book another one of those things you talk about, but don't really do?" She wasn't being mean or even rude. She was right. I talked about a lot of things over the years that hadn't happened.

I had begun writing in response to the sudden death of my younger sister, Ginna. Her loss had turned my world upside down and left me devastated. Through writing, I was trying to address the gaping hole in my chest and find a path forward.

My sister and I grew up in New York City; she was my only sibling and we had become increasingly close in the years leading up to her death. She was living in Nashville with her family, and I was in Southern California with mine. Ginna was beautiful, smart, wickedly funny, generous, and family-oriented.

I had ended up in California as an investor and cofounder of a medical device company that treats patients with obstructive sleep apnea (OSA). For those who aren't familiar with it, OSA is a serious medical condition that causes people to stop breathing in the night; the soft tissue in their throat falls back and blocks the airway, not allowing them to get enough oxygen. Over time, the lack of oxygen leads to cardiovascular and other health issues. There are an estimated one billion people globally with OSA, 80 percent of whom are undiagnosed—it's a serious problem. And in my case, it got personal.

A few years ago, I learned that Ginna had started snoring loudly, was tired all the time, and needed to take daily naps. Due to my work, I knew that snoring and daytime sleepiness were the leading symptoms of OSA. I talked to her about it on numerous occasions and sent her the name of a local specialist. Some combination of life being busy, disbelief, and little-sister-defiance kept her from getting checked.

Tragically, in December 2019 she died in her sleep. She was only forty-six. The autopsy showed that she had an enlarged heart and was in atrial fibrillation, which the EMTs could not stabilize. And while she may have also had other undiagnosed health issues, a cardiologist who reviewed the report told me that her condition was consistent with untreated OSA.

I was immediately struck by the searing irony. I had dedicated my professional life to helping people with OSA and the unthinkable happened. My company had treated thousands of people, yet I failed to help her. To make matters worse, a couple of months after she died the world went into lockdown due to the pandemic. It was a scary and unsettling time for everyone. And I was deep in the grieving process.

Despite everything going on, falling apart never felt like an option. I had to stay strong and keep my kids calm, optimistic, and focused on the future. In addition, my company was facing unprecedented challenges related to the pandemic that required a steady hand and clear thinking. I had to keep my head together, but my heart and soul were broken.

I knew I needed help and I needed to heal. I was fortunate to find an exceptional grief counselor. She listened, let me cry, be angry, frightened, or whatever it was I needed to be or feel on any particular day. Through our lengthy conversations, she guided me through the darkest days.

Around that time, I started writing daily first thing in the morning. I wrote mostly poems and found that the creative process helped me to make sense of what had happened. I was able to get clearer about my priorities, about who I was, who I wanted to be, what I needed to walk away from, and what was no longer serving me.

During that period, nature provided guidance, inspiration, and a form of escape. When I was outdoors, I felt free and untethered. It was where my spirit could sense the energy of other living things and connect deeply and organically. Every day my husband and I would go for a walk in our neighborhood. We live in a beautiful area filled with woods, citrus groves, and distant views of mountains and the ocean. Being outside and moving cleared my head and helped keep me calm and balanced. That unstructured time surrounded by trees, birds, and blue skies reintroduced a sense of wonder, possibility, and hope.

After a bit of soul-searching and a handful of meaningful conversations, I decided to organize my poems into a book. That's when my daughter asked the pivotal question and I thought, *I need to see this through*. I was reminded of what I said at Ginna's funeral. At the end of my eulogy, after describing her many accomplishments, her irreverent wit, and her inclination to celebrate, I suggested that "All we have is now. *Right now*. As in today. So, go carve out the life that you want and celebrate the milestones and people you love." This book stems from my own advice as I try to live more thoughtfully and deliberately.

MORNING LEAVES

Before sharing my poetry, I have a few practical suggestions based on my professional expertise and my personal experience. Hopefully they will empower you to make more informed decisions about your physical and emotional well-being, and you will find them helpful.

My first suggestion is tactical. If you know someone who snores or suffers from daytime sleepiness, encourage them to talk to their doctor. One in five adults have OSA, so it's likely you know someone who has it. Snoring is a warning. It's the body's way of sending out an alarm saying it needs help—something's not right. I have included resources at the back of the book (page 99) that can help with screening tools, finding a doctor, and understanding options. I hope my story sticks with you and when you hear the signs, you are able to help your loved ones.

The second is spiritual. Remember that all we have is now. Live your life. Take it seriously. Do what you want to do. Be who you want to be. Don't put it off. You never know what's coming.

And third, if you are grieving—be it from a death, a loss, a disappointment—I suggest the following:

1. Find a counselor, therapist, or wise friend to speak to; someone who will listen and can help you make sense of the situation and your feelings. Understanding the

context, your reactions, your vulnerabilities, and your resources is invaluable in healing.

2. Engage in an artistic endeavor. Art allows you to wrestle with a situation and process it by turning it into something else—something you have created. It provides a unique way to look at a situation, roll it around, and then use its energy to move you forward. It also provides a welcome escape in which your intellect can relax and your soul can do the talking. It could be writing, sculpture, painting, or dance—whatever medium you enjoy. For me it was writing and collaborating with Kelly, a painter.

3. Go outside. Spend time walking, paying attention, and absorbing all that exists around you. Movement, fresh air, and beauty are great gifts—they can heal and inspire. They are free and accessible to everyone and often overlooked.

MORNING LEAVES

The next section of this book contains my poems. As I mentioned, they were written in the very early mornings of the pandemic when the world was especially quiet and still. In the quiet, I listened to what my spirit had to say and I found that it wove together things I was feeling with what I had seen on my walks. What emerged was a series of botanical metaphors that allowed me to express myself in a way that I found helpful and fresh: I could see myself through a different lens and assess things in a new light.

I think there is something to glean from reading the poems straight through, but it's up to you. I envision the series as a journey through an enchanted forest or an imaginary garden where there are lush grasses, blooming flowers, and ripening fruits. But be warned, there are also sharp thorns, hostile creatures, and a raging fire that you will need to navigate.

The poems have their own language, a code of sorts. I believe the key is to listen—not just with your ears, but with your whole being. With your body. Your instinct. Your soul. You know when you know. You know when it's true. Just listen. See where it leads you.

MORNING LEAVES

It's time now.

Come join me in the garden of

my imagination.

Today I am a plum tree. My little white flowers
scented and fragrant. My crooked, knobbed joints
carrying ancient, generational slights. Enduring
year after year. My fruit, each a little piece of my
heart, may at times be hard, at times soft and
mealy, or dripping with sticky-sweet juices. But
sometimes, just sometimes, a delightful balance
that causes everything else to go quiet and fills
your soul with a song.

MORNING LEAVES

A baby pea shoot. Bright green, alive, awake,
fresh, new, eager, sweet, growing, growing, growing.
Full of health and bursting with life.
Here I am ready to go. Ready to take on the world.
Unfurling, stretching, reaching for the sun.

MORNING LEAVES

I am an oak tree—tall, deep, rooted. I know who I am.

I am clear and strong. I am rested and well.

You may lean on me.

I am not going anywhere.

MORNING LEAVES

Today a lemon tree. Bright in the sun. Fruit everywhere.
Happy offerings. Yet, I have sharp thorns tucked under
my leaves that may pierce. And if it's not time, my gift
will not be easily forthcoming. The twisting, turning,
pulling that won't make it feel like a gift at all.
Some days I'm a little tougher, a little less generous.
Biting and tart. But give me time and sunshine,
and my generosity flows. There's nothing quite like
my shiny green leaves and bursting yellow
against a cobalt blue sky.

MORNING LEAVES

Beautiful. Quiet. Sculptural. Blooming in the sun.
Flowers out on angled branches. Stillness. Warmth.
Cared for. Tended to. Appreciated. Glorious.
Resting and able to soak up the sun.

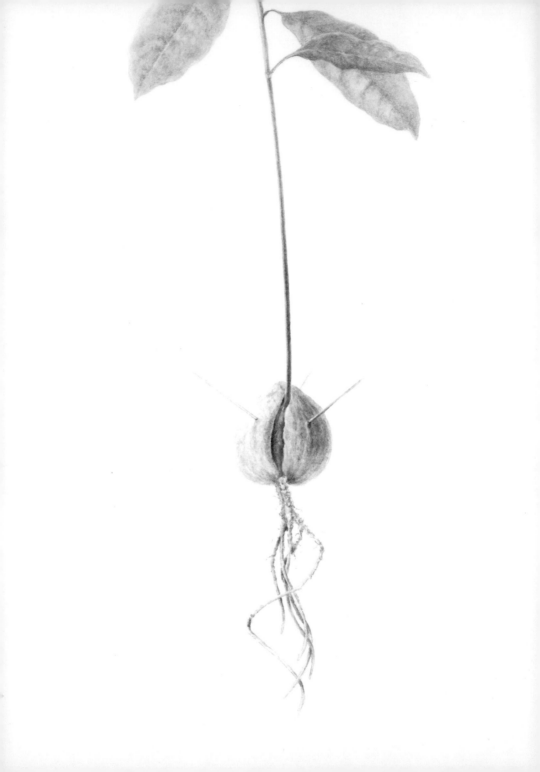

My heart is an avocado pit pierced with toothpicks,
hanging in my chest. Sprouting, extending up and
out. The stalk and leaves headed up to the sky.
Right out of my chest. Like *Jack and the Beanstalk*,
climbing up and up. Seeking the heavens, truth, and
a quiet respite on the white clouds.

I may look scrappy and weak, but have you seen my fruit?
It is round and full. The end, a crown and color from ruby red
to peridot green. The real magic comes when you open it
and see the glistening seeds. The richness of garnets.
I offer it to you. Something to delight in, share, savor.
It will give life and joy and healing.
It is here to be adored, tasted, and appreciated.
A jewel on a velvet pillow.

MORNING LEAVES

I am gnarled and sturdy and old.
And yet there is a newness in my fruit,
my green leaves.
My vines have been trained along wires
cascading out over the horizon.
I reach, grow, nourish, intoxicate.
I am open and sense the truth.
You feel the truth. I know you do.

ANCIENT PINE

An ancient pine in the deep woods. In a dark and angry place.
My needles are pointed and my boughs are strong.
Stay away. My claws are out. My defenses up.
Fierce. On guard. Ready to fight—defend—protect.

Deep rage. In the darkness. A place I must visit on occasion.
The pines around me are tall and strong and will be by my side
when the red-eyed wolf returns. My sentries. Standing up
to the darkness. The wolf will thrash and slice and holler, but
I will not break.

I may quietly retreat to the pinnacle and look out
to the clear sky and take in the cool air.
Yes, it is raging below. Yes, I am deeply grounded.
And yes, when it is too much, I must seek solace in the stars.

Hot pink with a yellow center and tiny pom-poms
flirting. Flitting. Garish. Overdone. Showing off.
Seeking attention. The ridiculous hibiscus.

But wait, a thread of envy. A dark line that cuts
deep into my well of insecurity.
Oh jealousy, you are cruel.
Name it. Own it. Be generous.
Tell her how marvelous she really is.

MORNING LEAVES

Overwhelmed, underconsuming, overconsuming.

Ablaze with inadequacy.

Covering my canopy with fiery flowers to divert and dazzle.

I bloat. Distend. Massive limbs crack and fall.

Out of balance, out of whack, lacking peace.

The breaks and stretch marks heal and scar, but they are still there.

I know where they are. I must cut back, prune, moderate.

Trust there will be enough. Trust I will be cared for.

Easier said than done in this over-irrigated world.

MORNING LEAVES

Raging fire. Whipping winds. Choking smoke.
I am scorched. Blackened. A searing gash within.
I am down. Flattened. Breathless. Felled . . .

And then a small voice, from the kitchen. And by
combination of instinct/will/miracle, a green sprout
pushes its way up, through the ashes.

MORNING LEAVES

A snake in the grass. Sinuous. Sinister.
Unpredictable. Remember it is there. In the grass.

You have such trouble remembering, as we know.
Beware the rustling in the leaves.

MORNING LEAVES

Today a cactus. The kind you see in Westerns.
Big, spiky, majestic. Yet inside, quite lonely. Alone.
Thorns on the outside to shield the soft flesh within.
Guarded, buffered, distracting to ensure that you
don't see the ache. But it's there. Inside the tall stalk
and into the big arms. In the beating sun and the
clear cold nights. By itself. Occasionally putting out
a beautiful flower to invite a bluebird to come sit
on its shoulder. To be together for a bit.

I am a skinny palm on the cliff's edge.

Heavy winds beating on me day after day, pushing me to their will.

Bending, flexing, enduring.

I am marveled at for the shape I take on.

Arched and contorted. Distorted by the tireless assault.

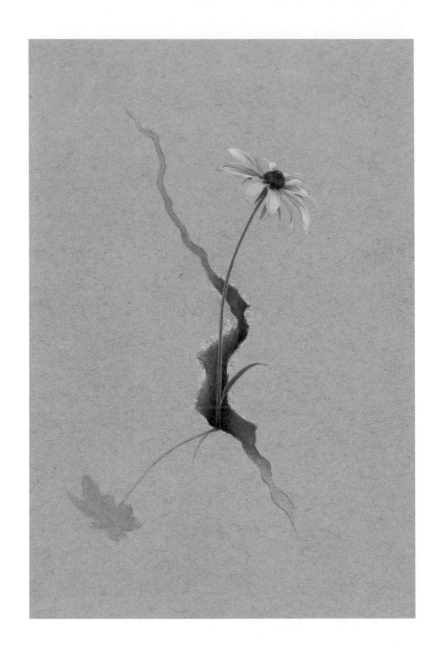

MORNING LEAVES

BLACK-EYED SUSAN

Oh, really?

You thought you could keep me down by
covering me with inches of concrete.
I will crack your confidence and rise up
right through the middle of your nonsense.

53

MORNING LEAVES

Strong, powerful, full of goodness and grace.
I will lead, solve, and keep my head held high.
Over evil, injustice, and fear. Steady and even.
Truth and honor. I understand.

I am in a field filled with breezes and sunshine.
I am pushed in the waves.
I can relax into the swell. I can float, dream, rest.
The flow is rhythmic and natural
and will carry me through the day.

MORNING LEAVES

A small, dense fir covered with snow. A cardinal
flies into my boughs and lands. Tucks her wings under,
and nestles in. I will protect you and keep you
warm and safe. You are welcome in my arms and
I am happy to see you. My mother would say
you are an angel. Maybe so.

MORNING LEAVES

Simple, strong, proud. Brave together, banded and deep.
Protecting little creatures and delicate sands below.
We are tenacious, ferocious, sharp. We are filled with beauty
and wonder as we wave at the open ocean and her fickle winds.

Rough and latticed. Leathered and aloof.
Lost in a tangle of oversized leaves.
I may appear dull.
There is nothing to prepare you for the splash
of color, light, and love you will discover within.

MORNING LEAVES

Intrepid, hearty, optimistic. Listening, feeling, sensing, knowing.
An awareness, empathy, and acceptance of all that is.
My stem buried deep in the rich, dark soil.
Embracing, warm, multidimensional.

Quiet now. There is no hurry.

We should linger here for a while.

Today a buttercup.

A touch of optimism.

A tiny mirror of the sun.

A needed ray of hope.

MORNING LEAVES

A thick stalk. I look up to the sky with my flower.
Petals swirling in pinwheel patterns.
Stocky and furrowed, but velvety and tender beneath.
Able to nourish. To be hardy. To flourish.
To take care of myself. To take care of others.

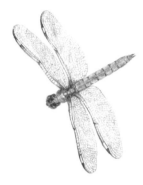

Today a morning glory. Blooming, stretching out, meandering along fences; tenacious, bold, able to give, hold on, weave around, get to where we need to go.

Come along now.

A birch in the deep woods.
Still and quiet.
Beautiful. Peaceful.
Full of wonder and grace.

A pine on my side lying in the deep snow.

A deer curled up on one side and a squirrel on the other.

Their snug bodies in tight circles. The warmth of their backs against me.

I feel their aliveness, their calmness.

We are connected for this time.

Connected to something else altogether.

MORNING LEAVES

I am a magnolia tree. Tall and strong and luminous.
My leaves are shiny on one side, suede on the other.
I am a pavilion adorned with glorious white flowers.
Come in, join me, we should celebrate.

Today a redwood. Christmas Day. Peace and wellness.

Happy, grateful, present, and clear. Whole and content.

The goodness of the earth, the sky, and the stars

runs through my enormous body. My trunk,

a conduit for mystery and joy.

Delicate, fragile, sweet scented.

Propped up with a tether of raffia.

An arm around the shoulder of this willowy, elegant guest.

Her annual, enchanted visit, too brief.

MORNING LEAVES

A lesson in patience. Slow, steady, not to be rushed.
Little by little, inching up. Bending this way and that
depending on the light.
And then finally, with bated breath, an explosion.
An eruption of blazing color. Big, brash, and extravagant.
The prize. The trophy. The gold ring that drives the carousel
of expectation 'round and 'round.

I am a gingko. A little whimsical. Lanky and fun.
A beautiful silhouette. A dash of pretty. A pinch
of magic. A butterfly or a heart or a dancing fan.
It's all there. Shimmering in the light. Filled with music.
Twirling in the universe. Twinkling and gay.

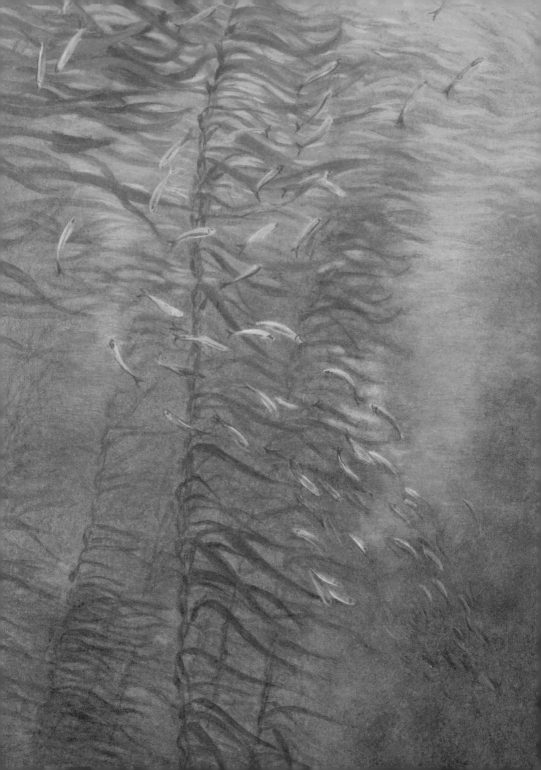

Giant kelp in the South African Ocean.

Tall, mighty, part of a fairy-tale forest under water.

Under the waves, under the crashing,

under the noise, the people, the trouble, the cares of the land.

Down here swaying, shifting, flickering in the light.

Glimmering sunlight slicing through

bringing brightness and splendor.

Away from it all, dancing with friends.

Enjoying being alive and strong.

Arms up, hips swaying,

feeling the groove.

MORNING LEAVES

Today a fern. New Year's Day. Quietly sitting in
the shade under the eave of a momentous year.
Resting, contemplating, assessing.
Appreciating the cool, damp moment
before the wheels start turning and the year takes off.

MORNING LEAVES

Trees talk underground. Root-to-root. Connection. Communication. Warnings. Knowledge. What do they share? What do they know? What would we learn if we could hear?

MORNING LEAVES

CONCLUSION

My poems were written in 2020 when the whole world paused. They fell out of the haunting quiet, the human standstill, the electric blue skies. It was an unusual time when many things slowed down.

The plant metaphors I discovered in those milky early mornings allowed me to express things I otherwise had trouble communicating. Writing was liberating, and I enjoyed tapping into the more artistic side of myself. The process created space for elements of my subconscious and my soul to drift up and out.

At first, I typed up and organized my poems so that I could give them to my children. Later, I realized that I wanted to share my writing with other people. I wanted to be known, understood, and heard; but I felt vulnerable and feared being judged. There were days that I considered abandoning the whole project. It was tempting to retreat into the dark woods where I would be protected, shielded, and out of sight.

Eventually, with my daughter's words in my head, I made the leap and sent my work to some friends. I found that instead of being critical, many of them pointed out which sections were their favorites and explained why. They told me stories and revealed things about themselves. The result was a series of wonderful conversations that led to deeper connections—the kind of connections that I craved and helped me feel more whole.

Losing someone you love raises all sorts of questions about meaning and the value of things that once felt important. There are times that Ginna sits on my shoulder and tells me that I'm focused on the wrong things and steers me in a different direction. She reminds me of what is truly important— our family, our friends, integrity, and being true to ourselves. I am trying hard to listen, to pay attention, to honor her and myself.

The creation of this book has allowed me to process what happened, to understand my strengths and limitations, and to get clearer about my priorities. In sharing it with the world, I hope that it will also support you as you reflect on these topics, so you are better able to care for yourself, enrich your life, and heal from your losses.

MORNING LEAVES

RESOURCES FOR OBSTRUCTIVE SLEEP APNEA (OSA)

AASM Sleep Education is the online patient education resource of the American Academy of Sleep Medicine. https://sleepeducation.org/patients/

The American Academy of Dental Sleep Medicine offers an online resource for patients. Learn about signs and symptoms, find a healthcare provider, and learn about oral appliance therapy for snoring and sleep apnea. https://www.aadsm.org/for_patients.php

ProSomnus Sleep Technologies is a leading brand of intra-oral devices for sleep apnea and snoring. The website makes it easy for patients to learn more about sleep apnea, snoring, and how to find a provider in their area. https://prosomnus.com/how-it-works/

Additional resources can be found at www.laingrikkers.com

ACKNOWLEDGMENTS

Thank you to my husband for his guidance, support, and care of the dogs every morning so that I could write. To my son for always modeling courage and tenacity. To my daughter for her kindness and beyond-her-years insights. To Mark and Lolly for their unwavering strength and love. To Elizabeth for holding my hand and gently guiding me back to the light. To Shelly and Veronica for all the tools they shared. To Mom for showing me how to be brave and take care of others. To Dad for believing in me. To Jim for being there every day. To Steve for all he's done. And to my grandmother, Nana, for instilling the evergreen value of art, prayer, and family.

Thanks to my friends, especially Tucker, Ia, Anna, Shilpi, AmyK, Trish, Tim, Carrie, Paul, and Lindsay, who encouraged me and patiently helped me work out the *why* of writing this book. To Len for his leadership in OSA and endorsement to speak up. To Mel and Antonios for their artistic suggestions. To Kam for asking about my spirituality at just the right moment. And to Linda for giving me the confidence to keep going.

And finally, thank you to Katie, Brian, and Angela—all part of the universe's daisy chain that led to this book being published. A special thank you to Leigh, for seeing what was possible, making me feel safe, and nudging me to dig deeper to say what needed to be said. And last but not least, to Kelly whose talent, vision, and enthusiasm brought my words to life and who, throughout the process, generously offered her wisdom and friendship.

Photo: CeCe Canton

ABOUT THE AUTHOR

Laing F. Rikkers grew up in New York City, attended Harvard College, and received an MA in psychology from Columbia University. She has been a medical device investor for most of her career and is a founder and the executive chairman of ProSomnus Sleep Technologies. She currently lives in Southern California with her husband, children, and dogs. Visit her at www.laingrikkers.com.

Photo: Winter Caplanson

ABOUT THE ARTIST

Kelly Leahy Radding grew up in rural Connecticut on the edge of a state forest. She honors the natural world she loves through her art. She finds all aspects of nature interesting subjects for her paintings. Animals, plants, butterflies, rocks, the sometimes overlooked, and the minute details of nature are to her an integral and necessary part of the whole. "My intention is to have my work create a connection not only to the physical beauty of the natural world that I love, but to reach a deeper understanding of our own essential connections to nature, to our own stories." Visit her at www.kellyleahyradding.com.